JUPITER MOMENTS

poems by

Barry Ballard

Finishing Line Press
Georgetown, Kentucky

JUPITER MOMENTS

Copyright © 2023 by Barry Ballard
ISBN 979-8-88838-170-0 First Edition
All rights reserved under International and Pan-American Copyright Conventions. No part of this book may be reproduced in any manner whatsoever without written permission from the publisher, except in the case of brief quotations embodied in critical articles and reviews.

ACKNOWLEDGMENTS

Special acknowledgement goes out to the following publishing houses who have included some of these poems in their chapbook publications

1. Snail's Pace Press; New York; 2000

2. Creative Ash press; 2002

3. Bright HILL Press; 2003

4. Finishing Line Press; 2003; Ohio

5. Pudding House Publications; Ohio ; 2006

Publisher: Leah Huete de Maines
Editor: Christen Kincaid
Cover Art: COVER PHOTO OF "EL CAPITAN" : by Barry Ballard. Winner of the 2007 PARADE MAGAZINE photo contest; selected out of over 62,000 entries
Author Photo: Barry Ballard
Cover Design: Elizabeth Maines McCleavy

Order online: www.finishinglinepress.com
also available on amazon.com

Author inquiries and mail orders:
Finishing Line Press
P. O. Box 1626
Georgetown, Kentucky 40324
U. S. A.

Table of Contents

PART ONE: GREEN TOMBS TO JUPITER

CONDITIONS
green tombs 1
hate-crime 2
landings 3
spill 4
heaven like shopping carts 5
this island earth 6
ansel adams 7
clearing an intersection 8
psychology of a pyromaniac 9
the jumper 10

ALIENATION
navigating this dome 13
quarrels 14
envy 15
returning invisible 16
moorings 17
sexual gravity 18
gone before they knew him 19
the span of one life 20
norsemen 21
taking an apartment 22

HOPE
our inability to explain our appearance 25
symmetry 26
one night a man determines not to die 27
breaking free 28
the edge of wilderness 29
ghosts 30
waterworld 31
jupiter 32

PART TWO: A TIME TO REINVENT

adam 35
with the sails down 36

between his feet 37
social security 38
cutting coal 39
half way 40
industry's children-moscow 41
on the loss of his wife 42
rough magic 43
main-sail 44
his rearrangement of room 45
poems 46
last breath 47
a time to reinvent 48
crossing the river 49
pools 50
ghosts 51
backing up 52
birth and rest 53
rowing 54
michigan october reunion 55
for burweed 56
the first law of nature 57
a mirror speaks 58
sleeping against her mother 59
a lunar landscape 60
mars 61
host galaxy 62

PART THREE: FIRST PROBE TO ANTARCTICA

CIRCUMSTANCE

first probe 67
a suicide 68
an interrogation 69
erosion 70
the fishing trip 71
dinner alone 72
creation's mistake 73
gary died 74
body 75
returning through the drift 76
even 77
in his image 78

DEFINITION
evolution/voice 81
quasars 82
mark's view 83
manya 84
tree-line 85
first morning 86
windows 87
a clear season 88
thatch work 89
during the snap back 90
reduced to sound 91
antarctica 92

PART FOUR: PLOWING TO THE END OF THE ROAD

EARTH
plowing 97
poplars at night 98
autumn 99
the fringe of color 100
the clearing 101
thatchwork 102

FIRE
first song 105
isaac 106
the sacrament of fire 107
writing through the ashes 108
from dust to dust 109
host galaxy 110

WATER
evolution/voice 113
visit of light 114
pools 115
navigating the storm 116
tidal wave 117
the equation 118

WIND
first kiss 121
from a flicker of silverweed 122
the prophet 123
a lunar landscape 124

oh red sky 125
the end of the road 126

PART FIVE: A BODY SPEAKS THROUGH FENCE LINES

a body speaks 129
the theater after the storm 130
an open mind 131
being flat 132
blue screen 133
the fall garden 134
rowing 135
howler monkeys 136
mending 137
god at I-20 138
after the rape 139
the garden 140
contemplating extinction 141
another gethsemane 142
after migration 143
reclaiming one's self 144
body glowing 145
no world 146
a wisp of green-gray 147
sunscape 148
drinking from the shoreline 149
birch trees 150
longitude 151
fence lines 152

To my most admired friend, Samar Reine.

And to my most honorable son Jamison.

PART I

Green Tombs to Jupiter

CONDITIONS

GREEN TOMBS

There are no green tombs here, where bodies wrap
their last words into the earth for children
to read the scattered symmetry, their blend
of wisdom and weed. We only react to something felt in the vertebrae, stacked
quarrels from the blank concrete that pretend to involve these places we imagine
when a buried voice slips out from a crack.

And we stretch our pain with pennies on our
eyes and our frame bent over like statues
blistered white, like soldiers covered over
with guilt or the feeling that they're cowards,
afraid that there might not be a rescue,
a reckless chance to shake the world sober.

HATE-CRIME

She spun on the apex of her fragile
morality, screaming like the last breath
that can't find an explanation. And death
wasn't forgiving with its waste and vile
display that colored her hands as they filled
themselves with what memory she could compress
into this narrowing ache. And the rest of her life emptied where the blood was spilled.

And she imagined that her son stood up
from the history still left in his body,
Asking to finish the life he'd begun.
Concrete shook beneath her, and lightning struck
From street lights as she folded restlessly,
Without room for the officer's questions.

LANDINGS

He sat next to someone (It could have been
Anyone.) and talked of how recliners
Rock life aircraft, the movement he preferred
For good landings. His furniture would end
Up much lighter now, helping him contend
With the gathered surroundings. It required
A table that wouldn't have to answer
For too many empty chairs or lost friends.

He mentioned how Alzheimer's had taken
His wife, how his x-rays showed vertebrae
Fused like fossils without insulators.
And you could see how his life was shaken,
Like an ancient pilot who's lost his way,
Searching for another navigator.

SPILL

There was a floating scar on the ocean
and it warped the sound like a hole centered
in a beautiful voice. You always heard
things about the urgency of fuel, one
bid for power that coated the eardrums
and watered the eyes. And even the birds
faltered at how beaches had been disturbed,
how tar knurled questions-marks in the sun.

We wondered how long it had evolved like
this, how it could compel us to net seals,
cover our hands with pitch and set them off
like torches welcoming the pain of light,
welcoming our lost ancestors who feel
this deeper shame and contemplate this loss.

HEAVEN LIKE SHOPPING CARTS

By tomorrow you'll be gone and they'll be
Sifting your brain for the sanitary
Land fill. Homeless refugees will carry
What they can of you, those bits of debris
That seem worth keeping. It's your chance to see
Their world with its exclusionary
Borders that outline a cemetery,
With street signs to imprint each casualty.

And you'll realize that death is a swift
Equalizer, that the outcasts do rule
Heaven. And your hope becomes nothing more
Than something thrown to cover you, a gift
That reads like a parable about fools
Who'd rather sleep when their own conscience roars.

THE ISLAND EARTH

On this island they don't understand why
You boil everything or add iodine
To the water. Your system is inclined
To reject the seasons and prophesy
About the cold intrusion like bone-dried
Words in the desert, Rod Sterling's last sign-
Post up ahead where the words on each line
Are bleeding from the carbon-monoxide.

But you've told them there won't be a surprise
Ending, like the time someone had all those
Books but broke his glasses and couldn't read.
We've stopped reading anyway, as if eyes
Were burned out from the inside, or just closed
Enough to keep the outcome guaranteed.

ANSEL ADAMS
1902—1984

> *There is too much clear sky and clean rock in my memory to wholly fall into self-illusion.*
> —Letter, Oct 9, 1933

What upsets me most is the way birds skip
Along concrete or walk the median
With the same vacant outlook as unmanned
Pedestrians, death's open membership.
The way a mother can dissolve and sip
Her life away, waiting while her child stands
Next to her searching beyond the flatlands
Buried with traffic and life without script.

Maybe that's why "clean rock" sounds attractive,
Something pointing beyond the photograph
Where the artist lets it speak for itself.
Maybe there life could be less reactive,
Less an illusion, where rivers are half
Themselves and half our blood—spilled like snowmelt.

CLEARING AN INTERSECTION

Street lights burned like torches while someone stood
Naked, screaming at an intersection
About how no one would pass, about some
Of the pain in his life and how things could
Have been different. A girl, just past childhood
Herself, stood nursing an infant with one
Breast exposed, wondering about the outcome,
If insanity could do any good.

She watched while they cuffed his hands and covered
Him, holding him down while they drove away.
She noticed how she didn't disapprove
Of what he'd done, how his words had smothered
The noise of the city, how fate can trade
Places with you, till someone makes you move.

PSYCHOLOGY OF A PYROMANIAC

If it's psychogenic then would he
have included grass fires to erase
the weed inside our monuments? Let's face
it, war never does that. It desperately
keeps us desperate, our children afraid we
might see what we've made of them. And the space
we end up with asks us to hide and paste
eyes over our eyes, and bleed our bodies.

We wonder why they, with match in
hands, are not running away but watching
blue flame burn off the petrified landscape;
like a small child huddled back in a dim
trough of wood, fumbling with what each day brings,
the twigs and dry leaves his fingers have raked.

THE JUMPER

It's simply a matter of perspective.
Among those in the streets I'm seen as just
Another jumper, waiting for a gust
Of wind to take me where something outlives
The sirens, ghosts, and chatter. They forgive
Themselves for saying I couldn't adjust,
For judging me immoral. They discuss
My fate as if they knew the way I lived.

But from on this ledge the voices never
Reach me. There's silence when the body rocks,
When the conscience reels again and again.
The air seems somewhat cooler whenever
You try to breathe. You imagine the shock
Of absence, the blood spilled all around them.

ALIENATION

NAVIGATING THIS DOME

For a lodestar, I'll use the beggar slumped
in the drunken sleep under the overpass,
circled by a tight orbit of ground glass,
stray dogs, and loose debris. He doesn't hunt
for answers there. It has more to do with
waiting for the boiling core to burn out.
You need those chiseled lines that speak about
the storms in his life, the way the clouds drift.

And so I move, having read of Mark strand's
"city of domes", the search inside the thick
bottle that can't ever find solutions,
a space hidden from skies of polished sand
where the map in someone's face seems to stick
against the flow of speeding confusion.

QUARRELS

After all these years and still an island-
like yolk of floating contradictions, from
what you see and what they see in you. Some
imagine it as ocean where the sand
and saline wash against the feet and hands,
keeping features smooth and filling eardrums
with some kind of universal rule spun
out of membrane that burst when time began.

But who notices when the first shallow
shock of pain wrenches the young liver, stirs
the milky sight with brittle distortions,
chips of shale up under the skin that show
themselves late as some kind of cancer,
strange quarrels that can afflict anyone.

ENVY

You can argue against evolution
And even make an emphatic statement,
A walk into the ocean with legs bent
From the strain of standing up against some
Of the meaning that came with the sand. None
Of it matters when it's the argument
Of body before water broke, a sense
Of "return", life measured in split-seconds.

But sex is still a "Prime-Mover", even
Though division hasn't set the penis,
Split the fingers, or opened a belly
Full of memory that remembers when
Envy had more to do with those things missed
On dry land or left floating in the sea.

RETURNING INVISIBLE

Nothing simple about dialectics,
the "in-at-the-eye" and "out-by-the-pores"
way of testing what we see. And before
you're done with this last internal critique,
you'll hear words like "betrayal" and "deceit"
from an ex-friend while his hand explores
frustration up some woman's skirt. And you're
left reframing things your system secretes.

The way streets seem empty when you enter,
how buildings are mocked-up props or just doll
houses where people couldn't stand unless
they stood like someone else. The curvature
of the earth so pronounced that your exile
leaves you only the narrowest access.

MOORINGS

After so many years, the moorings break,
something undiscovered where the conscience
gets pinched. It appears to be an accident,
the snap of case-hardened metals that shake
loose the tethered lines that accumulate
and test these battered hulls. You hear comments
about who's to blame, blistered arguments
that peel like paint and make the body ache.

They can only see you as another
man trying to wash cold rust from his face,
a pool of gray light lost in deep water.
At times, you even read the seas backward,
question the luck of wind, and find escape
a blind chance of what each sail can offer.

SEXUAL GRAVITY

Our loose choices and words were charcoal marks
Across sidewalks, experiments that we
Never returned to again. And sin freed
Us in its paradox, like modern art
Through the interpreters eyes. But things start
To gravitate over time and recede
From stronger centers, answering the need
To fill corners, and settle tight remarks.

We confused it with recovery, as if
We healed ourselves and conquered seasons like
Tempests that kept us feeling incomplete.
And exposure peeled certainty in stiff
Questions rising like glaring sheets of ice,
Darker than charcoal, weighted like concrete.

GONE BEFORE THEY KNEW HIM

I always imagined them saying, "He
Had everything". And that's the real problem,
Their perception (or the lack of). It's come
Down to this: a man who lived for twenty
Years in the country makes a casualty
Of himself and wraps bandages in one
Broad sweep across his ears and eyes. And none
 Of his thoughts escape for others to see.

So absence equals death and friends will speak
As if they knew the life he had, as if
Something in the rain (promised tomorrow)
Closes like a curtain where nothing leaks
Out from yesterday, nothing carries its
Dark memory, or resonates in sorrow.

THE SPAN OF ONE LIFE

Like one of those outdated suspension
Bridges where they run cables through the ends
Of your fingers and tightly attach them
To your brain. Everything you overcome
Or almost reach qualifies at least some
Of its capacity, whether you'll bend
And hold up under the stress, or contend
With cracks from the heated earth or loose tongues.

A few friends might wipe their fingers across
A faded postcard and talk about those
Days when we all worshiped the engineer.
And they'll question the dark water you've crossed,
How the current's hanged, or the way blood flows
Against itself when choices aren't that clear.

NORSEMEN
(The Confusion of Two Thousand Voices)

Or one voice from two thousand years ago
That points you this way. Spectators tell you
It's illusion or myth, the residue
That accumulates on tombstones this old.
It's just a boat-shaped grave out of control
And grown-over with what you're going through.
You don't notice it isn't moving, due
To dark water, thicker than green meadows.

And there's noise along the coastline, the sound
Of dialysis machines filtering
The blood. Someone saw too much inside you,
Something they questions, like the movement bound
Up inside, everything, shape disturbing
Shape, splitting the opposing molecules.

TAKING AN APARTMENT
(where the windows face the south wind)

I thought of mimicking that strange culture
that writes prayers on cloth and activates them
by hoisting flags to the wind. You pretend
that they go straight to heaven but I've heard
wind in the foulest places, dark textures
for clouding the content, a bitter blend
or hate, waste, or apathy. Demons end
up altering the original words.

Or even worse, the whole thing gets blown back
in your face where you breathe in what you just
breathed out. You stand at the mirror and ask
how in the hell did the image get cracked,
and what's the answer for saving enough
of this flesh and blood to smooth out the glass?

HOPE

OUR INABILITY TO EXPLAIN OUR APPEARANCE

Sometimes action is more like erosion
With patterns shearing off you like limestone
Or granite. Scientists and friends are flown
In to investigate the damage done,
To see if you're worth saving or someone
Simply gone away. Everything you own
Is catalogued as if it was the stone
Of body, particles once gathered from.

And you know there's no answer for why you're
Starting over again. It's like trying
To explain mountains, the way they can change.
If they could, they'd ruin asphalt to restore
The landscape, thick arguments applying
Logic to high winds, slope, ad pouring rain.

SYMMETRY

This body's stretched with its patchwork tilled so
deep that even friends (who stand back in clouds)
say they witness the betrayal that's plowed
through the tight symmetry, the overflow
of neighboring swamps that cause the saplings
to fold their roots, and each explanation
to drop like yellow withered leaves unstrung
from this choice and poisoned imaginings.

But if I've already raked the dry leaves
into fires and accepted the charred
consequences of what they call "mistakes,"
couldn't I plant a field of blossomed needs
and cultivate my time without them, far
from a need for fences with no escape?

ONE NIGHT AT A MAN DETERMINES NOT TO DIE

Do not go gentle into that good night. Rage, rage against the dying of the light.
—Dylan Thomas

Like birds that have lost their ability
To navigate, you're afraid of dying
In the north, sleeping or realizing
You forgot to listen, speak, or sing. Seeds
Of thought follow you to bed where they bleed
Through your eyelids without compromising
A single line. You manage the sizing
Of deep skies, noting what measurement read.

You tell yourself that you can never "not
Know" how to get out of this, even if
Water's ice of life refuses cover.
Maybe you've never flown or just forgot
What it meant when starting over like this,
Navigating like soldiers, or lovers.

BREAKING FREE

I'm sifting through my own memory the way
You'd sort through a closet of old keep-sakes.
You wonder sometimes how you'll ever shake
Loose from their attachment. But edges fray
Over time and you find out they don't say
That much about you anymore. You break
Free form yourself, determined to remake
The image before the chance slips away.

You'll hear others whisper about how they're going to remember you (the person
They once expected you to always be).
And you'll strike out at their elegy, tear
Pages apart, and let the words become
Nothing, just pieces of sifted debris.

THIS EDGE OF WILDERNESS

Street lights weep like willows and sirens scream
Like eagles bearing down on prey. Old men
Rest like owls in balconies and pretend
To capture secrets, those things caught between
The stairwells of concrete and life's routines.
And voices all but disappear or end
In rain or water. It all depends
On what's allowed to breathe or be unseen.

But sometimes you'll swear you observed yourself
Spilling voices down empty canyon walls.
You've learned to listen in this wilderness,
And recognize how the concrete can melt,
How, at times, even misery will crawl
Out from itself, like birds that leave the nest.

GHOSTS

When you have faults, do not fear to abandon them.
—Confucius

You don't ever completely kill or hide
From the ghosts. It's not like you could look out
Past everything and deny lines about
Your history. You'll catch them when you decide
To look in the rear-view mirror, cold-eyed
And asking. But you're done with all the doubt,
Comfortable with taking those risks without
A hint of fear or hidden compromise.

They're more of a standing reminder now,
Knowing innocence has its price to pay,
That it's better than something never worn.
They're fashioned less of substance anyhow,
So thin their shadows seldom block the way,
So frail that the shapes are sometimes torn.

WATERWORLD

The world is still covered in water
and you're waiting for something to surface
to stand on, maybe just a battered fist
of rock, shape enraged enough to occur
in this blank sea. Memory isn't bothered
by these lines on the horizon, the kiss
of space against space, holes we resist
when standing stark-naked and less secure.

You'll lay your wet clothes out under the sun
(which you believe to be a god) and watch
it pull pre-history from the shoreline,
even something you knew before, undone
by it all but given back, a small notch
in this new life that's used to measure time.

JUPITER

> *The abundance of carbon compounds on Jupiter, along with its wide range of temperatures, suggests that Jupiter may be able to evolve life.*
> —Terry Holt
> "The Universe Next Door"

I want a perfect body, an orbit
that's predictable, and under my left
arm, a massive vortex circling my breast,
large enough to swallow Earth and dismiss
the fact that it ever existed. It
will disintegrate things but the process
still leaves clouds swimming in carbon, a death
burning and freezing in salmon-pink mist.

And for twelve thousand miles my eye-sockets
will shower in thick seas that fill my womb,
metallic walls cradling the birth of charged
particles, spiraling embryos wet
With the space of this new birth, with each moon
Watching like assigned mid-wives standing guard.

PART II

A Time to Reinvent

Adam

Already teaching yourself pulsed rhythms
for opening and closing your mind shut
up in watertight compartments, the rough
edge of this new flesh learning to pretend
at a self refigured under this cowl
of sharp storms, these snake-bite-sorrows knuckled
up in a cauliflower of unwilled
traumas that only a god could allow.

The buried fist around your spine, deep swells
running their course as you till this crusted
ego into furrows like seeded earth,
unmapped gardens kneaded into hard-shelled
paralysis where the water runs red,
where conscience arrives and wrestles with birth.

WITHOUT THE SAILS DOWN

I can hear the ocean roar inside her,
her thin hair weaving another sunset
and the sight of a lone mast circumspect
and tipping (because she's swallowing word
for word of this argument she's taken
to bed). And her grip on the fitted sheet
makes me wonder if I could catch the weak
side of what she lets escape, something foreign

in her embrace while I'm kissing her breasts,
when we convert ceilings into skin-pricked
arrangement of still water, her disease
wailing like the distant creak of one death
after another seeping through the thick
woodwork of our floating lives, our histories.

BETWEEN HIS FEET

There's a man weaving baskets with his feet
and he's smiling at me like the razor
blade he holds between toes, severing more
away from me than that wide brittle reed
that needed trimming (as if I were disarmed in the moment like a brother). I
wonder if he sees how much has gone dry,
how much webbing has tightened into fists.

Something exists between us where the frayed
off waste separates in strands, something old
in the folded sleeves tucked into sleeves,
something that has erased our distance, waved
at us with open hands and clenched the holes
in his strong shoulders till each finger bleeds.

SOCIAL SECURITY

I'm supposed to take a number and stand
over there next to the young man with barbed
wire tattooed around his neck. He guards
his opinion by keeping the wasteland
of his collar pushed up around this fence
he's strung between us. And the screaming child
gets passed from mother to grandmother while
we move like dumb cattle without defense.

And I can hear the shame of all that history,
the gas chambers, the fate of one woman
muffling a child's hunger against her breast.
I can hear voices counting inventories
of shoes and gold teeth, all these voices jammed
inside, until the speaker broadcasts, "next."

CUTTING COAL

Sometimes the air's heavier than "chokedamp"
(what coal miners call carbon dioxide),
and the sky hangs like a blinding landslide
snapping the sprags, the whittled Will that can't
keep the dust from accumulating or
vent the increasing methane. And you know
that one wrong spark sets the culm to explode,
the waste we buried or simply ignored.

And at five miles down in our carved out
rooms, we stare at each other in twisted
black-face, peppered masks that vision rescue,
young boys calling for their mothers, the shouts
of panic from those who knew better, dead
men waiting, lungs heavy, their minds confused.

HALF WAY

The toughest things I learned from off the streets
were from the girls themselves who hollered
obscenities in their silent transfer
from rape or abuse to ice-cold concrete
and the red brick of semi-locked up
world where the casualties walked the halls.
And they opened themselves to the slow crawl
Of their childhood coming back just enough

so that they could still keep one hand tightened
in a fist, holding the world at arms length
so that nothing could smother or reach them.
And they sang like wild birds that were threatened
and saved at the same time, a song that sank
their hearts and never escaped the system.

INDUSTRIES' CHILDREN: *MOSCOW*

Sometimes smeared clouds of our own breath condense
above our heads and wash us with the same
pollution that caused our children the pain
of deformity, withered left hands clenched
so tight they disappeared. And while doctors
know that fingers burned off in fires
of needed industry, they still require
tests and peek into their mouths for answers.

You'd think they were looking into the wide
end of a telescope, tapping on glass
to stir the nebulous fragments stored there.
And you can tell from their soot-covered eyes
they didn't expect the songs floating past
crooked teeth, each note tweezered and stripped bare.

ON THE LOSS OF HIS WIFE

When most of the bitter grief has left you,
the only objectless thought that remains
is the sinking cold disguise of this chained
pool of fragments, icebergs hiding their view.
But friends still imagine they know your shape,
even though now you wake without fingers
(an unexpected sheared-off cliff), and you're
lost to sort photos or pack things in crates.

And even though they sit in the same room,
they can't tell you've drifted for miles, buried
in a strong current that covers your legs,
their hurried steps to places you assume
still hold her, places where voices carry
across each wave of the crusted landscape.

ROUGH MAGIC

His forgetfulness is simply our way
of walking through the snow-covered lessons
(which he taught me) of an appreciation
for Nature and the jarred questions it raised
when wildlife kept screaming from the barb-
wire fence. And we keep cutting things from red
plaid clothing and leather, prayers instead
of rehearsals where we step from the guard

of this familiar place toward broken
ice refrozen into jagged teeth, whispers
of things evaporated years ago.
And there's something there that says, "I've seen him
today," something you can't really measure,
a rough mixture of bare twig, thistle, and snow.

MAIN-SAIL

She raises and pins one side of her blouse
like the quiet flicker of a main-sail
caught in dead air space, a place that fails
to offer relief. But when asked about
the surgery that removed her arm or
the injury that shouldn't have cause it,
she lets loose of each word as if the tip
of fate was rising up from the seafloor.

And her self-acceptance and battened strength
make me wonder about this stall in her
history, this trap of night with floating stars.
And nothing seems to have hindered the length
of her reach, not the worn varnish, obscure
landscapes, or if the hull's battered or scarred.

HIS REARRANGEMENT OF ROOM

He created a wide space for his last
conversations (swept clean from losing his wife
to Alzheimer's). And I took a childlike
risk and entered that pitch black room that passed
rest and unrest for something in-between.
There were muffled tremors while I waited
for my eyes to adjust, for one small thread
of shape that could answer that silent scream

of questions he kept hiding in his face.
But there never were answers to explain,
or truth in the accidents of wordplay.
Just the distinct sound of the folded brace
And leg of a hospital bed, the pain
Of no sound when she finally slipped away.

POEMS

It can sound like a reality marked
across reality where you might read:
"The chemicals she received were earmarked
for cancer but swept through the flowing reeds
of hair, the soft budding fingernails." You
know she's sleeping in the next room, her bald
head camped with stuffed animals. And you use
everything you can, like "Promise calls

the sun sitting on the mountain, flooding
the sky with color." And you find ways
to hold the metaphor, believing this pain
isn't the infinite tunnel that brings
the last light, with the girl who died yesterday
—waiting, repeating your daughter's name.

LAST BREATH

Her slow words didn't mix, mince, or matter
except for what was between them, except
for knowing he was the last one to let
her go and the first one to mis-take her
sleeping. But she wouldn't let herself be
taken by Reason or religion or
rooms that smell antiseptic-white, where doors
become tunnels or faces you can't see.

Instead it was just a feeling pulled from
the pocket of his rough hand, the courage
of starting against those who disbelieved,
demanding death lose itself and not come
between them, where even now the eyes rage
against this in dreams of their young bodies.

A TIME TO REINVENT

The highest human purpose is always to reinvent and celebrate the sacred.
—N. Scott Momaday
1969 Pulitzer Price Winner

My curled body has been heated and cooled
so many times that even the last
yellowing scrap of surety whirlpools
away in nothing but wind. That pre-cast
shape that was clinging has become a quick
evaporation, an atmosphere against
the window where you can look straight in. It
takes courage to look, to "reinvent

The sacred" from as far back as Saigon,
or when you lost a friend, or when your son
stopped speaking. I guess it begins in the space
you cup between now and then, from napalm
to computer networks and the handgun
showing up at school pretending to be fate.

CROSSING THE RIVER

She had chosen this remote spot in her
history to lie face down (but not sleep),
cupping her arms with limestone and broad sweeps
of sand that sent leaves over stacked towers
into blubbing swells. Her invitation
(though silent) kept circling in the current,
urging my cautious steps over sediment
that filled her voice with sharp punctuation.

And she separated her opinions
like the cottonwood seed and yawned in proud
whirls that spun in shadows from my gait.
But of what she measured as the outcome
of the matter, I couldn't say, or how
much the encounter had altered our fate.

POOLS

For a brief moment, I'm prehistoric,
something I've found under the microscope
in the gum of water, a bubbled yoke
of slime teeming with motion. Its mystique
captures me, but for others it doesn't
matter, as if their world was covered
in dense cloud where something couldn't divert
them of pluck them into vacant fragments

of space (the ice age we once heard about
where the burst of our civilization
was split into pools with deepening rifts):
one with horns, one without; one with legs, one without; one with consciousness, one without; one
with humanity, and one without.

GHOSTS

> *When you have faults, do not fear to abandon them.*
> —Confucius

You don't ever completely kill or hide
from the ghosts. It's not like you could look out
past everything and deny lines about
your history. You'll catch them when you decide
to look in the rear-view mirror, cold-eyed
and asking. But you're done with all the doubt,
comfortable with taking those risks without
a hint of fear or hidden compromise.

They're more of a standing reminder now,
knowing innocence has its price to pay,
that it's better than something never worn.
They're fashioned less of substance anyhow,
so thin their shadows seldom bock the way,
so frail that the shapes are sometimes torn.

BACKING UP

Don't expect me to throw gentle words. I'm
trying to heal myself with magnets, fry
the migraines into blank Reason, excise
the smell of gasoline with hard sex blind
enough to keep me reading Braille lines
about starting over without space. I
can't get past this blur where lights circumcise
the darkness but still amplify the crime.

And I've never seen a whole face escape,
just amputated eyes that got used up
or swallowed by absence and its disease,
the same one that seeps like a slow heart-rate,
backing me up against my past enough
to prick the lungs when I struggle to breathe.

BIRTH AND REST

I think it was more than just emotion
that saw the sun dripping out of my heart
into that pregnant swell of landscape hung
like birth and rest, breaking each sound apart
and swallowing the receding notes. I
imagined it a cold experiment
in death, reminding me of someone who tried
just earlier to build an argument

which he expected could trick a god
into confusing life with afterlife,
where the sun might suddenly rise and melt
away his years like dew off seedpods,
like pain at the edge of conscience where bright
sunsets bury their figure, taste, and smell.

ROWING

Each word dropped like a wooden oar into
smooth water, twisting its restless version
of a new start into vortexes spun
like knives through your reflecting solitude.
And with each breath, you strained against the pinned
spine of what someone measured as balance,
the frictionless space of blind circumstance
that's always needed grease or metal shims.

And even the sand that had been bleached white
on the other side couldn't hold your print
or generate an occasion for rest,
as you unburied yourself fin the flight
of new steps through blinding light that squinted
back in hushed voices affirming your theft.

MICHIGAN OCTOBER REUNION

My hand opened up like the seeded far
end of my father's garden where Poplars
were dying along the fence line with their
arms stretched out in stark need. And the nightmares
curled up in my fingers (which I brought
with me) peeled like white birch around each knot
of anxiety, with each Maple swept
up in red shadow, leaves dripping with sweat.

And when my brother took it (for the first
time in twenty years), I felt color burst
behind my eyes and wondered what we could
hope or expect, like my father who stood
covered in questions raking his fingers
through the sprawling plants that were growing there.

FOR BURWEED

There isn't a day without a corner
on it, a place covered in rock-hard sky
where cellophane leaves simply amplify
the fact that our rush slit the jugular.
And the person I just passed had his shadow
pulled up over his head, which made it
comfortable for us (rituals that permit
movement without sight, a blind polio).

So why is it that the warped sidewalks bleed,
that the fleshy earth curls where it's been
split? Why is it that the memory stays "green,"
arguing its disturbance like burweed
that sticks to your clothing, your frayed problems,
and a "self" that's determined to be seen?

THE FIRST LAW OF NATURE

You take the time (even in high winds) to
rake up the knotted shape of yourself like
dry leaves that have scattered around drainpipe,
soaking up the roof tar and gravel spewed
out around your face. And you wrestle through
the repetitions harboring the right
of "self-preservation inside the tight-
fitted gloves that often times smother you.

But the conscience wakes when the edges lift,
when something from Poe settles like "madness,"
the hurried stride of fumbling against
time with storms of matches cast at the risk,
folding it all back in racing warm breath
that rises like bold shapes that we invent.

A MIRROR SPEAKS

> *... what remains of the self unwinds ... where the unsayable, finally, once more is uttered...*
> —Mark Strand
> "In Memory of Joseph Brodsky"

Is this the epitome of conscious
humanity: man "reflecting," the man
of glass? And if it is, then how much sand
has been polished out of the fever pressed
into the tablet across from me, where
an arm is scratching, (where something of Locke's
wax tablet is more than "imprint"), where cropped-
out phrases are strung in genetic pairs?

Maybe he struggles (as I do) against
the ripple of light across this fixed plane
of shape, lapping the loose place where I stand.
And if consciousness is a poison meant
For us, then I can understand his pain,
His unwound words: "I am. I am. I am."

SLEEPING AGAINST HER MOTHER

The mother's right arm cradled Orion,
with Cassiopeia at a standstill
wavering at her left. Her breath circled
the empty space with wisps of scarlet, strung
like shaded nebulas, the clouded views
of a new world beginning, bright palettes
of color and reflective drifts that swept
the line of merging shape between the two.

And the infant's fingers were curled out
of its only memory of this rush
of blood beating like pulsars never seen,
an identity in dreams and deep sound
floating like embryos caught in the hush
of her waist and the heartbeat in-between.

A LUNAR LANDSCAPE

You might hear the drums at night and pull down
a smooth moon and press it against your cheek,
rolling the brittle mountains with their bleak
forecast against the shape of your frame has found,
planting deep craters where there once had been
eyes, threading the history of casualty
from every dry river through the deep sea
of your hearing, its hidden vibrations.

And later, in your shallow sleep, you'd dream
of the dark side of your life, the side that
screams protest against the infinite space,
a random map of meaning that's unseen
for a reason, scouring each impact
with wind and fine dust to sculpture your shape.

MARS

I always expected you to find me,
hurling your coned questions at me sideways
with glancing blows that cut my cheeks. You stayed
there, under my skin (that circulates free
of heat) measuring my wide scars that you
called "similarity," manipulating
red dust till it scattered light. The fading
quakes left us restless, splitting views into

secrets where I caught you listening at my
four yawning spouts. You wondered how the stones
were sorted when you split open my fists,
when you stretched out my one-hundredth outcry
of a self, searching for germs microbes,
or a beating pulse frozen in my wrist.

HOST GALAXY

If a star hangs like a spiked blade (someone
said it did), then I wonder if it could peel the Earth like an orange; the livelihood
of our planet, our best history, spun
out in curls of nebulous dust, exposed
for the taking. The meat of our fervored
morality wedged apart, the unheard
reasons of our existence just shadows,

black holes, or dark matter. And the random
spit of seed scattering us like charred fragments
of diffused light, hot stars in the Virgo
Cluster's ripe spiraling sea, split-seconds
of graphite glowing in the firmament
like deep blue souls of what we used to know.

PART III

FIRST PROBE TO ANTARCTICA

CIRCUMSTANCE

FIRST PROBE

When the earth is tempered, compressed and cooled
in the heavens like something somber
and inanimate, I wonder if we'll
be photographed, or spectrum smudged and framed
on someone's laboratory floor, each hue
of color speaking of how we were conquered
by our own base elements. They'd peel
back the layers, speculate about the chain

of our history, if it was sung
or written, if their probes could still find it
in the chipped palms of our carbon fists, carrying
off the frozen samples where the small sum
of our "soul of ideas" would be cupped
like breathing ashes in their stainless steel hands.

A SUICIDE

If the earth filled itself with warm water
and slit open its wrists (say along some
narrow green peninsula), I wonder
what she would see during the last seconds
of breath, what would matter, what would appear
in the swirling red sea? What memory
of triumph would melt like golden wax tears
from the candle she'd lit? What lines would she

highlight in her favorite book of glacier bays,
what signs of mist in streaming waterfalls?
Who would she call? Who would she trust with this
imprint she carried of "all living things,"
this sacrifice in a porcelain paved
altar, begging for hope—begging forgiveness?

AN INTERROGATION

I hear a human voice in the motion
of landscape, a voice of rotting disease
and beauty saying something about real
transcendence. It carries me from daylight
to its shadow of trees where I'm bound from one
to the other, where it slides its thin reed-
like fingers against my ribs (to get a feel
for my heart rate and breathing). And I fight

my imagination, wondering if I'm
the pagan sacrifice hung with the cattle,
fish, and foul. Or if this might be brutal
interrogation, where choking vine-
like voices point toward more than winter kill,
swirling up rage in fistful after fistful.

EROSION

I returned for innocence, for condonation
from the architecture of the house
where I was raised. It stood with teeth cracked,
gums peeled back at the soil, and eyes burned out
with stains reflecting a sea of diffused
forest across the street. The framework frowned
in broken columns and laps of scars confined
with layers of emotion (its shape drowned

in shades of chipped paint). And it questioned me,
asking for its own escape across
this cold grassy expanse of forty years,
trying to mend the sting of injury
hidden in the attic, hidden in the crawl
space where the erosion is more severe.

THE FISHING TRIP

Before we slipped the boat, I dipped my hand
into all that dripping silence that stirred
the water, trying to make first contact
with its quiet power before reflection
spoiled its innocence with trees, before sand
was lapped up in ripples of scorn. I heard
angels speak before that dawn, voices back
against those shadows tugging at the sun.

I knew our conversation would unnest
like spools of tangle line unkept for years.
(And after years of absence, saying "I'm
your son" demands some kind of forgiveness.)
So we took our time, trolling along sheared
drop-offs, gauging our chances on both sides.

DINNER ALONE

Even when the last space is cleared for me,
there's something left from the casual sweep,
from the distance in the twisted stare squeezed
outside of sight. My consciousness repeats
its story, knowing I've never sat down
together with complete self-acceptance,
knowing this difficulty that surrounds
me in low light when reading my hands. I glance

at the commentary of ruined woodwork
on the floor, or the accessories
of atmosphere hung like three-dimensional
abstracts. And the piercing answers "hurt"
(just a little) as my glass filled like
a blue ocean: halfway empty, hallway full.

CREATION'S MISTAKE

My friend is dying and stifled flowers
are bending in the garden, cupping sin,
fear, and regret from the silent power
of drought that takes them without a crosswind
of debate or cunning. The already
imagined absence raked beneath their feet,
deep mendings written across in valleys
erasing each shade of history. They reach

for the next world behind the drawn blinds,
beyond fingers curled in creation's mistake.
They ask to be remembered for the green
outside the seeded rows, for the stray vines
tangled in thought but able to create
beauty outside symmetry and routine.

GARY DIED,

and everything he touched was vacuumed clean,
the tile counters wiped with pure alcohol
so even if bent into the blank sprawl
of sunlight, you couldn't find the last gleam
of his fingerprints. His business was sold,
partitioned, and renamed, his collectibles
donated for tax write-offs. (Each armful
of his "designated space" boxed like souls

of who he used to be.) His wife remarried
after four months and started creating
her own new memories, while others decayed,
like Reason erasing the myth. And we
expected the "conqueror worm,"—but not the sting
of "invisibility," hidden in the clay.

BODY

Know in the sharp spires broken off stars
falling out of eyesight, sticking in tear-
duct glands like slow burning crystallized shards
of salt. Know in the slated atmosphere
emerging in the sweat-glazed paste coating
the limbs of landscape, the skin of ocean
sinking in the palm of our hand. Erosion
is tensioned against reproductive seed

in this mystery, in this density
of "matter" in blank space (the gaps between
the fingers, toes, and legs). Feel this universe,
this root of body inverted with weed
and beauty tangled in the sky, a stream
of knotted rivers where the lips are pursed.

RETURNING THROUGH THE DRIFT

She tells me (like Wordsworth) eternity
sleeps without motion in the womb, that birth
is like "sleep and forgetting," that even
in retrospect there's nothing to be grasped.
So when the doctor can see "nothing," we
don't need to split the world into raw earth
and Plato's "idea" extending tension
between the mistake, a dialectic flash

of beauty that's supposed to heal or rescue.
And I shrink from our argument that breaks
this time to sorrow, as we drive through this
season where cottonwoods fill our world view
with blankets of wind-borne seed, seed that aches
inside this flurry of accident and miss.

EVEN

He tells me his daughter has given up,
that she has settled for her wheelchair,
so he built her a pool where she can be
"even" with her friends, where their heads can bob
of laughter surrounding her as the sea
of embryonic fluid ensnares
her weightless legs. And he holds back enough

to keep from breaking to tears as he looks
at me as if looking into himself,
searching through his towering height and lean
physical strength for the answer to hook
the severed nerves of his mind together, for help
with the shiver when he pulls her from the stream.

IN HIS IMAGE

If the child at the end of the street
sits in the hand of God, then she's the pinched
blood vessel, the thick leather like scar. She's
always facing the swirled traffic, an inch
away from releasing all those prayers
folded in the pleats of her dress, staring
into a space that once filled her arms. She's aware
of more pain than she needs: that court hearings

are dressed-up lies, that visits from case workers
still leave the world created in tremors
of her father's image. And sometimes I
can hear her speaking in bright-colored
flags across the canyon of her sleep, words poured
like oiled paint cascading from her bedside.

DEFINITION

EVOLUTION/VOICE

Sometimes a conscience can swim like those first
stages of evolution where mystery
has yet to be sculpted out of the sea.
It may have nothing to do with your birth,
age, or the color of your skin. It might
simply be the confusion of music
with your logic, whale-songs waking the sleep
of predictable space in broad daylight.

But not every motion washes in tides
pulsing with the moon. Some are so random
that their rolling imaginations reach
meaning by swimming through starlight, which finds
more definition in warm drifts than one
firm step through litter scattered on the beach.

QUASARS

There is difficulty and benefit
in unlearning the matter that touches us,
in hypnotizing a contradiction
from its sharp bombardment of particles.
And then reaching further than what exists,
out toward quasars of exploding gas and dust
that sit on the edge of "beginning," those hums
in the radio telescope that fill

our contracting heart with one universe.
(Not the poet's heart but the temporal
fleshy organ beating down that towering
wall of proof we've been shouldered against
   since birth,
beating through self-judgment, beating quarrel
after quarrel, beating silence, beating…)

MARK'S VIEW

Just understanding Twain was difficult
(and it shouldn't have been), but the man seems
at ease in this water, in this routine
sea of shipwrecks wrecking others. He balks
at those porous islands floating like sponges
that soak up the bodies and the rotted
plank, warning me not to read the dead
biographies cast at our feet. He says,

"a man cannot be written," or condoned,
or excused, that we swim in our own deep
waters; and that a soul may or may not
be like the wind, but it's more than what's owned,
more than those buttons and overcoats that speak
in complex meaning all tied up in knots.

MANYA

> *We must believe that we are gifted for something and that this thing must be attained.*
> —Marie Curie, 1867—1934

These were "fairy tales," gingerbread workshops
full of luminous silhouettes bottling
the intense blush of earth's aura in steamed
capsules. These were "haunted dreams" where
hearts stopped beating, where fortune was blind when the prince
got killed by a horse-drawn carriage, when rough
edges were never soothed with a mother's touch.
This was destiny and Radium rinsed

From raw Pitchblende, an urgency buried
in the scar tissue of each lung, in nerves
burning like sails in her fingertips.
This was Einsteins "unspoiled" verse, a soul married
in the end to the revealing soft blur
of an x-ray, moving among the sick.

TREE LINE

In my father's world there is one field,
and one tree line working as a wind break.
On one side everything is planted in rows,
a penance furrowed like the scar tissue
cutting his lungs. His conscience is wheeled
from one end to the other, each mistake
measured with what he remembers, each stone
piled in altars for his god to review.

The other side's scattered in deep thickets
of briar and black locust that barely
let in light, an unnavigated space
he'll wander for days while his condition twists
sorrow like wild grapevine, with wind-blown seed
skimming the moist soil of a birthplace.

FIRST MORNING

There's an inscription inside that cloud hinged
on the horizon, sealed like an inverted
cuneiform wedged sideways into the earth.
It's written out of yesterday's deep-lying
faults, from the thirst of each mistake. And in
hours it will reach me as the content sheds
its color in streaming burn-off, each word
untangled in pure thought before dying.

And so I take what I can of it now,
and anticipate what I hope it can be
when it splits into a millennium
of suppositions, or when it somehow
concentrates its meaning into one key
embryo of dew, gleaming against the sun.

WINDOWS

On a bad day, I can hear the fire
consuming my chances to participate,
a blistering fury that suffocates
"figure" and "color" by stealing its tired
breath. I can smell a vapored hesitance
covering me in a bitterness of smoke,
knotting itself through each swallow in a choke
of fisted ash that's always imminent.

On a good day, the anatomy
and raw architecture of creation
stand like a rich dialogue of belief
passing through me, where words come back like
seed, saltgrass, or plaid cloth printed in thousands
of windows opened to possibility.

A CLEAR SEASON

If I should say what this winter's left me,
I won't mean the season. But I will mean
that something's been left, something just past
the seed of a second beginning, the saline
"bite" of something more than soul. Some say
the penetrating freeze was necessary,
that it clears a body of its own decay.
And so I embrace the green fragility,

the first stumble of my eyesight across
this rocky Martian-like landscape where red-
death lines the interior and the last
sound of distant grieving has already crossed.
I accept this remarkable emptiness,
these unpaired echoes streaming above my past.

THATCH WORK

I moved toward the standing dead timber,
the wooded Michigan landscape that could
never escape like a dying cold moon.
I entered as almost a child, almost
beginning with my memory wrapped backward,
wrapped like that thatch work of diseased
deadwood and dry leaf that last season had pruned
from stories; spilled tree line's endnotes.

And like a dying poplar I stood there
while neither of us spoke, while the disorder
of words stirred at my feet (which I arranged
and internalized). And from the repair
of their "sense of being," I remeasured
my fate: my springlike goals, my winter's pain.

DURING THE SNAP BACK

I can't help wondering why my longing to live forever has so abated that it hardly comes to me anymore.
—C.K. Williams, "Droplets," from *Repair*

I am a shrewd owner (I'll admit that),
the one listening to the words arguing
in my mouth, where the words listen to the ring
and pitch of what they "can" and "can't." I act
on whether I'll cup my bleeding hand
under the jeweled spill of water and light
dripping off the bent leaf (which snaps a tight
line of memory back to itself). I am

the one challenged to drink from this quiet
burst of fulfillment that has wrestled its way
past thick veins, speckled disease, and torn
holes where one can look straight through a
vignette of body, wondering at this peace that's made
both bitter and sweet, cradled in the storm.

REDUCED TO SOUND

I don't picture it singing or scattering
light so that it diffuses the hard line
and shape of its surroundings. I define
it as simply my whole sound replacing
me, a center in the traffic and noise
for a handful of listeners (some capsized
in words, others covering their ears). And I
will be in no particular place, yet poised

and still heavy with a pulsing substance,
thicker than the crawl of rain and just
as giving or dangerous. What a broad
spill of eternity I will make: those tense
moments of screaming from inside the rush,
or facing a landscape—standing in awe.

ANTARCTICA

> *The Wright, Taylor, and Victoria are the largest continuous areas of ice-free land on the continent. They are known as the "dry valleys," and geologists estimate that it has not rained or snowed there for at least one million years. The dryness also means that nothing decomposes.*
> —Sally Cole-Misch

I want my body flooded with six straight
months of daylight, my mind recentered
at a precise longitude, and across
my brittle chest, a beaded trenchlike scar
dry enough to preserve and dehydrate
every lost imagining. Their unheard
endings will float like islands lifting off
this wind-swept graying, like something nature guards.

And at the apex of my splitting free
and coming together, I'll launch my dreams
like calving icebergs floating northward,
with my skin breeding up brilliant algae
in yellow-green (the gold in the white out singing
like whale song echoing past my borders).

PART IV

PLOWING TO THE END OF THE ROAD

EARTH

PLOWING

I hid behind the clamor of thunder
peering timidly over its cumulus
shoulders, almost afraid yet drawn to trust
its broad proclamations. And I observed
nothing but a single man on a tractor
carving straight lines into the rugged
soil with the billowing dust animated
by his activity. And yet they were

at one in this simple practice of their
metaphysic (satisfied that the earth
can be just the earth), at one in that prized
calm just before the rain when the measure
of a day and its meaning is clear in the thirst
of body and the wiping of the eyes.

POPLARS AT NIGHT

It strikes me how everything remains green,
except these poplars that have been stricken
with their own early mortality (wind
breaks finally breaking up in the wind). They seem
unwilling to vacate this narrow band
of space they've shared with fence lines, and too quiet,
as if the meaning they tried to collect
was still hidden in the tilled pastureland.

But they still stand erect, depend on each
other, and contend with those rusting twists
of barbed steel at their ankles, disallowing
even one step from this quiet retreat
into turbulence, where memory is wished
into seed and the moon is bright for plowing.

AUTUMN

Writing it down years later has to be
enough, even though something is wanting,
something reaching from the memory of need
and affection. I see my father tromping
through the thick foliage or standing amongst
the trees, with the forest floor woven year
after year below our feet. I see us come
together with what I held inside (near

enough to understand that I still hold it
in some odd way, rewound and protected).
And I think he sees the same child, or at least
for a moment before he realizes
this is "now" and that what we expected
has changed—for as far as we can reach.

THE FRINGE OF COLOR

> *The inner essence of the Absolute could be reached by human reason because the absolute is disclosed in Nature.*
> —Samuel Stumph
> *On Hegel*

We had come across a place in the landscape
where you could know yourself by what was returned
over a steep pined valley. And my wife
asked, "What color do you see?" (knowing
that I'm color blind and that I reshape
the world in some odd way she can't learn).
And I told her that even without light
I can find the Absolute, that it brings

itself (or myself) to me without tinged
exaggerations. And I reminded her
about Frost's "leaf that lingered brown," and how
it was his thought that moved it, the outer fringe
of his late walk interpreting the earth's
color before it faded or fell to the ground.

THE CLEARING

I remember the place where the earth spoke
its mind, and not in the rush of pounding
waterfalls with words rolled up in a fist.
Not in the bend and roll of the river
where you can never quite know where words choke
away in the narrowing. Not in the spring
meadows where words sometimes sleep in the twist
of seeded grass curled and whispering skyward.

Bit in the shaded clearing of a deep
wooded range where I could tell all at once
that time had been at work, where the cast
of a struggle was settled in the steep
shadows and half-buried stones, in the slump
of timber praying—as I crossed its bedded path.

THATCHWORK

I moved toward the standing dead timber,
the wooded Michigan landscape that could
never escape like a dying cold moon.
I entered as almost a child, almost
Beginning with my memory wrapped backward,
wrapped like that thatchwork of diseased deadwood
and dry leaf that last season had pruned
from stories spilled in the treeline's endnotes.

And like a dying Poplar I stood there
while neither of us spoke, while the disorder
of words stirred at my feet (which I arranged
and internalized). And from the repair
of their "sense of being," I remeasured
my fate: my Spring-like goals, my Winter's pain.

FIRE

FIRST SONG
(Galaxy)

This is mystery spiraling out from my
body in wide streams of fragmented light,
the intention or the dream kept inside
of me that I could not contain. What might
I believe from these first stars and planets
spinning at my fingertips, so open
and wild from the fire and water that's swept
over me (over the year I can

barely remember, over the empty
black seas)? This is the mystery of their long
look back: reaching from their quiet hunger,
the silence behind their art, and the need
between us which has always been a song
or a poem, the "knowing" behind the words.

ISAAC

I've chosen the altar and lifted my
own body into the fire (I feel some
pride in that), the smoke rising in curled gray
filaments of who I used to be, blown
like Isaac's trust into the earth's blear-eyed
silent witness. And like that child, I become
the question reaching into my own flames,
believing that looking back through the once pure bone

can somehow redeem it. But in that wail
and sudden jerk back into my own grip
of covenant, I somehow feel relieved
in that heat against my face, in the stale
odor and cold ashes I will visit
tomorrow, firm in the sackcloth of history.

THE SACRAMENT OF FIRE

The fire had dissected his face: one
side smooth, one side scarred. And thought spilled in knots
from the isle between the two, from the dim
cavity of sacraments where his tongue
anointed each word with that baptism
of pairing the birth of light with the sunspots
of fate. And I accepted his gentle hymn
of conversation as a gift from someone

who had traveled so far in opposing
directions (the extremity of pain
and the beauty of his son's birth), that I
could only imagine his fate exposing
the gate of heaven, his body reclaimed
in pure symmetry—mirrored from side to side.

WRITING THROUGH THE ASHES

> *They are that that talks of going*
> *But never gets away;...*
>   —Robert Frost
>   *The Sound of Trees*

I want the victims of Auschwitz living
in the palm of my right hand and the plain
beauty of Frost's poetry as an offering
in the left. And I want to write the pain
of it all with my right, while the guarded
fingers of the other slide down the shadowed
edge, so that when I think of "discarded
humanity" or "gas chamber, I'll also

think of the "sound of trees" and how maybe
now their voices are together (in the bend
of their "knowing" and their almost resigned
dream of getting away). And even though
their names are marred, I'll hold them (and hold them)
if only for the span of fourteen lines.

FROM DUST TO DUST

From those we thought dead, there are voices formed
and leaking like swells of blue atmosphere
from the ion blanket that swirls in storms
to cover their face. They coax themselves from here,
where their stories cluster like proto-stellar
nebula filled with the ash and metal
of what they've learned. They burn like "early stars"
compressing the memory of their bodies, filled

with the bleeding radiation of their souls
peaking in ultraviolet, where they still
cling to that core of shape that mimics us,
expanding the reach of our dreams like "class O's"
(those supergiants), converting their cells of
Hydrogen to light in a bold, streaming rush.

HOST GALAXY

If a star hangs like a spiked blade (someone
said it did), then I wonder if it could
peel the Earth like an orange; the livelihood
of our planet, our best history, spun
out in curls of nebulous dust, exposed
for the taking. The meat of our fervored
morality wedged apart, the unheard
reasons for our existence just shadows,

black holes, or dark matter. And the random
spit of seed scattering us like charred fragments
of diffused light, hot stars in the Virgo
Cluster's ripe spiraling sea, split-seconds
ff graphite glowing in the firmament
like deep blue souls of what we used to know.

WATER

EVOLUTION/VOICE

Sometimes a conscience can swim like those first
stages of evolution where mystery
has yet to be sculpted out of the sea.
It may have nothing to do with your birth,
Age, or the color of your skin. It might
simply be the confusion of music
with your logic, whale-songs waking the sleep
of predictable space in broad daylight.

But not every motion washes in tides
pulsing with the moon. Some are so random
that their rolling imaginations reach
meaning by swimming through starlight, which finds
more definition in warm drifts than one
firm step through litter scattered on the beach.

VISIT OF LIGHT

There's something shimmering in the river
that doesn't belong to the river or
to me. It's something temporal that pours
itself over the surface in a quiver
of light, skimming the quiet boil and roll
of water through the canyons of limestone
and live oak trees. And when kneeling alone
at the edge of its body (swallowed whole

in the luminous drift), I can almost
feel the cooled remnants of last night's starlight
exchanging elements in the descending
layers of falloff, exposing the ghost-
like outline of each constellation to life
and its unwinding, its stall, its bending.

POOLS

For a brief moment, I'm prehistoric,
something I've found under the microscope
in the gum of water, a bubbled yoke
of slime teeming with motion. Its mystique
captures me, but for others it doesn't
matter, as if their world was covered
in dense cloud where something couldn't divert
them or pluck them into vacant fragments

of space (the ice age we once heard about
where the burst of our civilization
was split into pools with deepening rifts):
one with horns, one without; one with legs, one without; one with consciousness, one without; one
with humanity, and one without.

NAVIGATING THE STORM

And the dazzle
Of light upon the waters is as nothing beside the changes wrought therein,...
   —Mark Strand
   The Next Time

Our chance at starting over again keeps
staring up at us form the reflections
in the spill-water washing its pitch-like slum
over the sidewalks. And we lean or leap
across its direct path which has puddled
and become difficult to follow,
arranging our bits of cover below
the rains, cautious, sometimes at a standstill.

And our world keeps deepening below its
sheen, changing its meaning or rippling
into the mirage of the fixed structures
beside us. The very boundaries adrift
in a riddle we walk on: the window sills
broken, glass shattered, searching for the answer.

TIDAL WAVE

Imagine running toward water where gulls
are floating like loose-folded thought, where salt
seasons the pressing light. In one fistful
of shale and sand you've already been taught
the earth is alive, a violent womb
that shares your own history. And in just one
quacking drop of the ocean floor, the room
you expected for your next breath becomes

the tidal swells of her drawn belly, tossed
and heaving in three minute intervals,
her fingers raking through clouds uncurled
in brash expectation, her chest un-crossed
and thundering back at God in a spill
of echoes lost at the edge of this world.

THE EQUATION

> *The two Voyagers will coast through the void, murmuring quietly to anyone still listening… then wrapped in silence, they will lose themselves in the encircling wilderness of stars.*
> —Time-Life
> *The Far Planets*

There's something new, I think, in this gigantic
equation, something stretched from the thick
salty edge of the ocean and tethered
to the tail of our sagging history. (As if
it was trying to snap us back from our sleep
into its murky cold embryo.) And its
pressure will rip our bodies into pure
single-cell organisms, sealed moon-lit

bubbles of fragmented thought tugged by motion
and gravity until the questions we've asked
are launched into the mystery of endless sky.
(All drifting like Voyager satellites past our Sun
toward sister galaxies, the exploding gas
of nebulas, and the voice of light before it dies.)

WIND

FIRST KISS

> *The cosmic energy seems to be a purposive power contending with purposeless materials.*
> —E. S. Brightman

When we were the spark of pure thought before
the explosion (striking the flint or rasp
before the birth of oxygen), I wonder
why we didn't already sense the ruin
in the muck and matter waiting like a whore
with its lips painted. She wore a mask
that made us believe she was the thunder
and heat of galaxies, with the whirlwind

of streaming life behind her kiss. We tried
to tame her, waiting in her womb of "Mind"
and "Contemplation" to cover themselves,
walk out from her water with the earth dry
and waiting in its first second of "Time,"
waiting for the new mystery inside itself.

FROM A FLICKER OF SILVERWEED

Before I understood her grown body
(when she was just a small handful of sand),
I could imagine her sounds and pick things
up in the wind's velocity. And I
knew then the soft light in the silverweed,
and that the rain, the timber, the carved land,
all lived inside me. And even the evening
"mourn" of what she believed couldn't die

without first waking me and resting against
my chest, her body bare and leaning
between how far I've come and how far I
need to go, her lips the tonic and scent
trickling from the crest of each horizon, seaming
our thoughts together, preparing for light.

THE PROPHET

The wind came like a prophet to the end
of our street, calling us to our front doors
before ending its body into the stream
of our night. It disrupted our litter
of words (neatly piled like problems
to be collected, burned, and ignored),
scattering our secrets and self-esteem
into simple debris tumbling skyward.

It turned us sideways against our arrangement
of vertical landscapes, piercing us,
narrowing our eyes, and forcing our arms
to shield our arid tongues (as if it meant
for us to listen to our own frailty
caught in the whirlwind of erosion and dust).

A LUNAR LANDSCAPE

You might hear the drums at night and pull down
a smooth moon and press it against your cheek,
rolling the brittle mountains with their bleak
forecast against the shape your frame has found,
planting deep craters where there once had been
eyes, threading the history of casualty
from every dry river through the deep sea
of your hearing, its hidden vibrations.

And later, in your shallow sleep, you'd dream
of the dark side of your life, the side that
screams protest against the infinite space,
a random map of meaning that's unseen
for a reason, scouring each impact
with wind and fine dust to sculpture your shape.

OH RED SKY. . .

My crimson brother, how you comfort me,
listening to me bellow like October
winds about my small problems, while night-birds
cackle (as if my silent voice could breathe
up under their wings). Oh copper stream, my
sweet sister, how you delicately blend
our thoughts together, opening each of them
to their own dream and conquering the lie

that would have stolen their endings away
from the Heron guarding their sleep. Oh deep
blanket of earth, my autumn counselor,
cradling my shadow in the warmth made
from your own body of ashes, from the sweep
of your brittle tears off the cold river's shore.

THE END OF THE ROAD

Even though the last sunbeam has been swept
through the end of this road, there's something I feel
still with me in the image that reflects
back from the landscape of Maples that peel
their bodies apart and weep into the soil.
My own body believes its story, that even
the art behind me could possibly spoil
before finding a way to being again.

I look, with Frost, for as far as I can,
while all my understanding travels against
the stream, swallowing up the restless wind
and breathing it back: stirring the loose sand
up under the leaves, as f a path was meant
to be here, hidden under the praying limbs.

PART V

A BODY SPEAKS THROUGH FENCE LINES

A BODY SPEAKS

> *I feel a slippery self eluding me, gliding into deeper and darker water than I care to probe.*
> —Vladimir Nabokov

Someone better than me has just walked out
the back door where he sits on the patio,
having been almost mourned out of the shadows
learned from our conversation. It's about
pain tonight, or why he has to carry
all the consciousness for what it means
to be human. And his contemplation seems
so still that I know nothing gets buried,

and nothing boils away. His thought burns
like a blue flame skimming a half-full cup
or oil, where (try as I will) I can never
understand the content he discerns
from the space above that flame, or the build-up
on the glass diffusing his quiet glare.

THE THEATER AFTER THE STORM

Nothing ever made sense from the front row
seats, where you could stretch your legs across the grime
of earth's trenched gut, or where the trailing draft
of a passing car would suck the mind's leaves
into the traffic. Even when its shadow covered your eyes, there was nothing to align
the broken rows of picket fence. It gave half
a breath, its atmosphere too thick to breathe.

But from the back, the world stirred in its wine-like
watercolor, the blur of a soft drizzle
after all of that storm. Its calm wind
escaped the gripping squeal of sirens and moaned
like a child in a moment so still
that I'd swear the clouds rinsed the sky clear again.

AN OPEN MIND

Contemplation is the permanent lake
that started as a river till you dammed
it and watched the water rise. The brushland
of particulars are the trees, and the outbreak
of mistletoe and grapevine that sometimes
choke them. (Of course, the fallen dry leaves
are the pieces that didn't fit, the freed
ends of thought shifting in the open mind.)

And emotion trickles from the unguarded
edge as if truth had come to you as lightning,
rain, or hail and the winds that can sweep the slate
clean again. What can you do but simply
hold yourself for those moments so still
that even the Heron watch you—and wait.

BEING FLAT

> *It must be troubling for the god who loves you*
> *To ponder how much happier you'd be today*
> *Had you been able to glimpse your many futures.*
>   —Carl Dennis
>   The God Who Loves You

Being flat is something. It's as quiet
as the sleeping wild bird on the patio.
and it has a terrible meaning left
out like last night's news, or a portfolio
of photographs that can't be wished back. Even
a knowing word about the God of each
disappointment is nothing but a friend
explaining our loss in the places we reach.

It's something etched permanently inside
like that maze of scratches in the soft pine
desktop, where the past twenty-five years
cry out so many conflicting stories of why
tonight (of all nights) you ask for the signs
of "enduring", your reasons for having been here.

BLUE-SCREEN

After a while you realize
you're standing in front of a blank blue-screen,
reciting words about how you'll excise
the world's demons, and how your work will mean
something and make a difference. And then
you notice your neighbor isn't really
going to work, and that the couple at the end
of the street don't really argue continually.

You're struck with a lightning-bolt of awareness
that your convictions are nothing but a small
island. And someone has painted in
a landscape, and a poor attempt at inspired
humanity, while you slept by yourself
in a house that no one recognizes.

THE FALL GARDEN

We wonder about our reasons for being
here, why this square hole we have cut into
the earth has evolved into a bleeding
twist of stem, fruit, and weed (a soul removed
from its own symmetry by its random
search and retreat from light). We only react
to the hard place we breathe, leaving us stunned
into corpses where we amplify the facts:

that worms have eaten away the soft words
that grounded us, that our limbs are covered
in disease. And we return—complaining
of "life wasted," dreaming of the world
we planted, afraid of what's to be discovered
in our short season, in the holes we've been framing.

ROWING

Inside my father is the last vision
of water, a small lake of no consequence
in northern Michigan. His existence
rests somewhere between that place and the numb
reality of a cancer that grows
against his sight. We visit through Chippewa
skies, and warm our feet in bleached sand that crawls
deeper into the Pines and their soft shadows.

And it seems that our memory (our love
and regrets) always evolve to this:
a morning that opens before it has moved,
a mirror of forgiveness we're allowed to touch,
or the reach of our arms through the early mist,
as if everything was new ahead of us.

HOWLER MONKEYS

I feel my body vanishing in the green
Amazon water where even the Shaman
with his magic leaves can only glean
the endings of my dreams retreating (strands
of thought scowling like old howler monkeys
waiting in the trees for the skies to darken).
He rubs the fire of nettles against me
in a ritual of mystical invasion.

And I keep waiting for the jaguar
of his spirit-children who will lead him
to the hiding place of my remedy,
the invitation from Nature to breathe
something further back than human consciousness,
where even the dead—forgive themselves.

MENDING

> *Something there is that doesn't love a wall,*
> *That sends the frozen-swell under it,*
> *And spills the upper boulders in the sun;*
> *And makes gaps even two can pass abreast.*
> —Robert Frost
> *Mending Wall*

My son and I are working on dismantling
this barrier we've constructed for the last
five years. We'll chip at the mortar and pry
each stone from its ledge, slowly easing its bulk
then wrenching it to the edge of a ravine.
They always leave their winding scar-like path
before we send them over the edge like a lie
we don't care to remember or talk about.

And later (after he's already home
in his own apartment) I'll lay in bed
and feel my body ache: maybe because
of labor, maybe because the soul's alone
aching from something it gained, like when he said
just being with me counted and was always enough.

GOD AT I-20

God was wearing a pair of faded
blue jeans and a solid tee-shirt, screaming
at the blackbirds and smoke exhaust in the dead
language of some unknown tongue. And the steaming
rage of the place was running down his brow
and into his eyes as if the world
had wrung itself through his body, the ground
that he stood on, and his battered self-will.

And in one of those rare moments when First Cause
or The Infinite accidentally connects
(when a stop light brings you face to face), you'd
swear that this could be your own father
and that for one instance (while you both share
the same sky), you could be his only son.

AFTER THE RAPE

You are the freedom of open pastureland
sold and divided into duplicated
plots of texture scraped to sorrow. Each strand
of thought and segment of your history spread
to bleed in the sun with a number on it
(wounds without gauze lined up like a bitter
war's casualties). And your own slipping grip
of dignity afraid of the answer

in the unsettled dust, thinking: why
are we allowed to die like this, with our
unclaimed goals and a future we've never known
retreating like wildlife through the sky
and shadows, leaving our questions on their
battered knees searching—searching their way home.

THE GARDEN

Sometimes when downtown in the neon glare,
you can see things glowing in your body
that sunlight fails to detect, a layer
of someone else reaching (almost timidly)
for the blood-red roses on every street
corner. It's always the place where you turn
when the memory is fed, when the mind competes
for beauty were the hanging street lights burn.

And you know the air should be sweet with voices full
of the fragrance of civility, that the hands
soiled and reaching from the sidewalks should end
in bright blossom, elegance, and armfuls
of symmetry, and that the dying should stand
as if the sun was saying, "Let's start again".

CONTEMPLATING EXTINCTION

When the earth is alone (when it has left
the sound of everyone else and ponders
its own shadow in the abandoned depths
of evergreen), I wonder if the answers
hurt, just a little (the way that our's do)
when it remembers the almost passing stir
of beardtongue, the wormwood, and the blue-
green silverbush swaying in the coastal berm.

I wonder what it leaves to the walls
of darkness that surround it at night, what tears
of abject denial are still re-mixed
through the turbulence of waterfall,
its prayer showing up like an aurora
of northern light, a spectrum of its hope and fear.

ANOTHER GETHSEMANE

> *We haven't' too much time left to ensure that the government of the earth, by the earth, for the earth, shall not perish from the people.*
> —C. P. Snow

If the dying earth stood on its own mountain
(let's say Everest, without any water
or oxygen), I wonder if the glaciers
would thaw when it fell to its knees, if the winds
would die in the rain forest (collapsing
its failing lung). I wonder what secret
it would pray when looking out over the nests
of its next portrait, over the wildlife thrashing

through rivers, through foliage, or the salt
air above the sea. What would it deny,
argue, or hallucinate when the storms
gathered, when it lost itself in its own brawl
of thunder, begging God for clearer skies,
for a world it wouldn't have to mourn.

AFTER MIGRATION

The finer part of mankind will never perish. They will migrate from sun to sun as they go out. And so there is no end to life, to intellect and the perfection of humanity, its progress is everlasting.
—Konstantin E. Tsiolkovskii

When we look back from whatever we've crossed
and from the system where we've migrated,
how will we gather all our loose thoughts cut-off
from the earth's gravity? What narrated
songs of our history will we choose to reply,
as it transits our new landscape with the unused
color of our "purpose", the disarray
of its unbalanced carbons glowing, subdued?

How will we encapsulate the orbiting
soft voices still flowing in the oil-like
portrait of its half-lit face, where the memory
still tumbles and grows like the last defiant
species of wildflower, where even the soil
fights as if the future was still waiting there?

RECLAIMING ONE'S SELF

Sometimes reflection is more like waking
from the grasp of storm, like a funnel
of wind snapping your logic (taking
your thoughts and crushing them like straw pummeled
into timber's wrinkled face). And you think,
"My God, what am I to make of these lost
borders, what of this scattered debris linked
to my secrets and the range it's all stretched across?

The mind keeps ticking like someone's wound clock
that shouldn't be there, counting off the torn
pieces of yourself you lift from the rubble:
a frame without a picture, a locked
hasp securing nothing, and the worn
surface of a door—dislodged, without a pull.

BODY GLOWING

Today, in the streets, I will be the man
burning with my tattooed vignettes of framed
identity rising like rust-colored
smoke in the afternoon sky. I will move
with respect through my body glowing, crammed
inside the brittle bones where I explain
to myself this judgement for starting over
again. This will be the night I remove

his armor, his skin, and take him out
from the cover of his own canopy.
This will be the night that each star doubles
itself and looks into its own dying
face, spreading itself in spectrums of color
revealing each element of pain and trust.

NO WORLD...

ends without another one beginning,
carbon becomes electric. Concentrate
on oblivion and something still sings,
a vision of the unknown about to wake
from the heaving throw of the ocean, where sealed
microcosms of identity are etched
into single grains. This is why you can feel
the urge to start again, to move beyond your death.

And remember: Your body will always be
the riverbed of washed stones, the fusion
of weightlessness and gravity defining
itself through rain, through catastrophe,
and through the restless motion of hope wrung
from the river's flow, its stall, its windings.

A WISP OF GREEN-GRAY

When Orion transits tonight, I wonder
if I'll feel the tip of his sword creasing
my rooftop, or it the nebula breeding
new-born stars might initiate their obscure
beginning by sleeping in my bed. Light
that old is bound to leave something, residue
from a history full of shadows that moves
through me in an image that's almost lifelike.

There's something behind that green-gray veil
that is more than the "gleam" of his sword, an edge
that cuts me both ways and questions all my
long hours at his eyepiece, the pale
thin wisp of the person I could be, spread
from my troubled world to all his open sky.

SUNSCAPE

Sometimes you can hear the Sun after it
disappears on the western horizon,
whispering to the quiet ones inventing
themselves in sleep. There's a sense of shadow
and revealing light we haven't lived yet,
an almost muffled translation
of the important things we've lost in streams
of vapor and dust in the burnt-orange afterglow.

And we can only guess at the boiling
consequences that will erupt like plasma
in the chromosphere, the twisting vortex
of free choice and evolving Fate, folding
itself through so many layers of the life
we've chosen and the life we've chosen to neglect.

DRINKING FROM THE SHORELINE

Sometimes your introspection is no more
than sliding your arms under a calm lake
of reflections, prying up the trees, the four
corner of the earth, and even the timid space
of cloud and sky with your bare hands. And then
cupping the simple rare nobility
of their elements into a trickling blend
of scattered light, where you drink from their mystery,

Where a billion-year narration mixes
with the quiet flicker of your existence
(the meat and wine of your single day's
brevity), leaving you to no more than the edges
of where this thirst has gathered your attendance,
where tomorrow builds from what you take away.

BIRCH TREES

> *I'd like to get away from earth awhile*
> *And then come back to it and begin over*
> 　　　—Robert Frost
> 　　*Birches*

What are we but the waiting metaphor
of the forest in front of us, the trunk
of peeling white birch that's almost ignored
in the bleach of winter's whiteout. Our limbs strung
from the edge of the streets to the dark centers
of marsh and swamp where undressed life is teeming
in microscopic storms, where the soul enters
the fluid of body—the mind dreaming.

Our ideas of who we are seeping
up through the crust of our many years frozen
at our feet, reaching for the delicate
array of fern and evergreen easing
dawn's visit of light into shadow (blending
their imagery through the world around us).

LONGITUDE

A worn path from no particular place
carries me through a section of forest
I've never ventured, attaching itself
to my simple clear awareness of being
alone. It vacates longitude and waits
for direction as we travel, a few steps
at a time, into the contemplative spell
of trees—where their shadows have been bleeding.

And we wonder how we will fare in this
thicket of weightless thought, winding us
around giant elms or in and out
of the drift of water, where our minds enlist
the shifting light around us for deciding
at what to move, or what to leave untouched.

FENCE LINES

I imagine these last Poplars dying
for something, a martyrdom of fence lines
giving themselves away for the crying
loss of meaning in the yellow-green mind
of wildflowers and grain. I wonder
what they've seen when the air shoulders them
and darkens, when a harvest has been gathered
leaving the soil bleeding to start again.

I respect the part they've played, and how
our future has grown because of them. Their
bodies, brittle and cracked from when they've faced
the cold ahead of us, never allowed
the comfort of rest or sleep, and so aware
of our fragility and the turns of fate.

ACKNOWLEDGMENTS

Thanks to the editors of the following journals and anthologies where some of the poems in this collection first appeared.

PART I

American Diaspora (Anthology): Symmetry
American Literary Review: Ansel Adams
American Poets and Poetry: One Night a Man Determines Not To Die
Baltimore Review: Sexual Gravity
Barbaric Yawp: The Jumper
Beauty for Ashes: Ghosts
Chance Magazine: Quarrels
Concho River Review: Breaking Free
Explorations: Hate-Crime
Flint Hills Review: Our Inability to Explain Our Appearance
Hunger Magazine: Envy
Inconoclast: Moorings
Midwestern Quarterly: Green Tombs
Mind Purge: Taking an Apartment
Oxford Magazine: The Span of One Life
Paris/Atlantic: Heaven Like Shopping Carts
Pennsylvania English: This Island Earth
Porcupine Magazine: Spill, Waterworld
Raintown Review: Landings
Rattapallax: Returning Invisible
The Review: Gone Before They Knew Him
River King: Clearing an Intersection
Rockford Review: Gone Before They Knew Him
TMP Irregular: Norsemen
Twilight Ending: Navigating This Dome
Violence in America (Anthology): Psychology of a Pyromaniac
Weber Studies: Jupiter

PART II

The American Workplace (Anthology by Florida State University): Cutting Coal

Baltimore Review: Host Galaxy
Beauty for Ashes Poetry Review: Ghost
Birmingham Poetry Review (University of Alabama): Lunar Landscape
Comstock review: A Time To Reinvent
Cottonwood (University of Kansas): Main-Sail
English Journal (Youngstown state University): With The Sails Down, Rough Magic
Event (Douglas College): Backing Up
Florida Review (University of Central Florida): Poems
G.W. Review (George Washington State University): Adam
Ginger Hill (Slippery Rock University): The First Law of Nature
Half Tones to Jubilee (Pensacola College): Industries Children: Moscow
Illuminations (College of Charlston): Last Breath
The McGuffin (Schoolcraft College): On The Loss of His Wife
New Delta Review (Louisiana State University): A Mirror Speaks
Rio Grande Review (University of Texas/El Paso): Rowing
Sierra Nevada College Review: For Burweed
Talking River Review (Louis-Clark State University): Between His Feet
Trestle Creek Review (North Idaho College): Crossing The River

PART III

Chachalaca Poetry Review: Antarctica
Chariton Review: Erosion, Fishing Trip, During the Snap Back
Daybreak: A Suicide
Hazmat: Returning Through The Drift, Windows
Licking River: Gary Died
Mochila Review: Dinner Alone
Old Red Kimono: Creations' Mistake
Oregon Review: Quasars
Phantasmagoria: Reduced to Sound, Even
Porcupine Magazine: First Morning
Quarterly West: Evolution/Voice
Quasar Review: An Interrogation
Ratte: Manya
Rosebud: First Probe
REAL: In His Image
Ship of Fools: A clear Season
Sunstone: Tree Line
Taproot: Body

Westview: Mark's View

PART IV

Baltimore Review: Host Galaxy
Bayou: First Kiss
Birmingham Poetry Review: Lunar Landscape
Cide Press Review: Poplars at Night
Comstock Review: The Clearing
Eclipse: First Song
88: Visit of Light
Hollins Critic: Fringe of Color
Licking River Review: Plowing
Louisiana Literature: Navigating the Storm
Mochila Review: Dust to Dust
Nightsun: Sacrament of Fire
Prairie Winds: Isaac
Pudding Magazine: Flicker of Silverweed
Quarterly West: Evolution/Voice
RE:AL: The Equation
Smartish Place: Tidal Wave
Thema: Writing Through The Ashes
Valparaiso Review: Autumn

PART V

Tulane Review (Tulane University): Theater After the Storm
Medicinal Purposes: An Open Mind
Adirondack Review: Being Flat
Pudding Magazine: Blue Screen
Poem (University of Alabama): Fall Garden
Weber Studies (Weber St. University): Rowing
The Aurorean: Mending
Square Lake: God at I-20
Owen Wister Review (University of Wyoming): After the Rape
Out of Line: The Garden
Diner: Another Gethsemane
Mid-America Review: After Migration
Branches Quarterly: Howler Monkeys

Flyway (Iowa St University): Reclaiming One's Self
Poetry East (DePaul University): No World
Midwest Quarterly (Pitt. State University): Wisp of Green-Gray
Thema: Sunscape
Poetry East (DePaul University): Drinking From the Shoreline
Diner: Birch Trees
Adirondack Review: Longitude
Florida Review (University of Central Florida): Fence Lines.

Barry **Ballard** was born in Holt, Michigan. After returning from Vietnam, he studied theology and philosophy, receiving an M.A. from Texas Christian University in 1983. Barry Ballard's sonnets have appeared in *Smartish Pace, Rosebud, Hollins Critic,* and *National Forum.* Recipient of the "Explorations award for Literature" from the University of Alaska and the "Boswell Poetry Price" from Texas Christian University, Ballard also published five additional chapbook collections, four of which are award winners: *Green Tombs To Jupiter* (Snail's Pace Press Prize for 2000), *A Time To Reinvent* (Creative Ash Press Prize for 2001), *First Probe To Antarctica* (Bright Hill Press Prize for 2002), and *Plowing To The End of the Road* (Finishing Line Press Award for 2003). He lives and writes from Fort Worth, Texas.

www.ingramcontent.com/pod-product-compliance
Lightning Source LLC
Chambersburg PA
CBHW020233170426
43201CB00007B/410